Rumi's Four
Essential Practices

Rumi's Four Essential Practices

ECSTATIC BODY, AWAKENED SOUL

WILL JOHNSON

Inner Traditions
Rochester, Vermont • Toronto, Canada

Inner Traditions
One Park Street
Rochester, Vermont 05767
www.InnerTraditions.com

Library of Congress Cataloging-in-Publication Data
Johnson, Will, 1946–
  Rumi's four essential practices : ecstatic body, awakened soul / Will Johnson.
      p. cm.
  Summary: "Poems and commentary that open the door for a new generation to experience the ecstatic and embodied spiritual truths contained in Rumi's poetry"—Provided by publisher.
  ISBN 978-1-59477-310-5
  1. Jalal al-Din Rumi, Maulana, 1207–1273. 2. God (Islam)—Worship and love. 3. Spiritual life—Islam. 4. Jalal al-Din Rumi, Maulana, 1207–1273. Poems. English. Selections. I. Title.

  BP189.7.M42J655 2010
  297.4'46—dc22

                                                            2009038611

Printed and bound in the United States by Berryville Graphics

10 9 8 7 6 5 4 3 2 1

Text design and layout by Priscilla Baker
This book was typeset in Bembo, with Centaur used as a display typeface

To send correspondence to the author of this book, mail a first-class letter to the author c/o Inner Traditions • Bear & Company, One Park Street, Rochester, VT 05767, and we will forward the communication.

CONTENTS

A RELIGION OF INTOXICATED LOVE AND ECSTASY

R eligion is always born out of a moment of radical insight but then all too often devolves into a system of rules and beliefs that turns the original insight into an event to worship rather than an experience to re-create. "Organized religion," says the Swiss psychoanalyst Carl Jung, "is a defense against having the religious experience." The religious experience is everyone's birthright, but paradoxically we brace ourselves against having this experience. We hold back on the inner forces and energies that, yielded to, give birth to the soul, and we often tragically refer to religious text and tradition to justify this denial.

Introduction

Jalaluddin Rumi—the great thirteenth-century Sufi poet, mystic, and originator of the dance of the whirling dervishes—began his life within the folds of orthodox religious tradition, but ultimately he had to go beyond the accepted practices and prescribed forms of prayer in order to have the religious experience for himself. To truly grow in soul, he found that two things were necessary: you have to surrender to love, and you have to dissolve the self that keeps that love contained:

falling in love
took me away from academia
and reading the Koran so much

just like that
it made me crazy and insane

I used to go to the mosque
to throw myself on the prayer rug

Introduction

and cover myself in devotion

but one day love entered the mosque
and spoke to me:
"o wise one,
why do you stay stuck
inside this house of worship?
what you need to do is break free
from the bondage of self"

The path of embodied love, which takes you beyond your self, is a far more potent way of inviting the religious experience than is compliant participation in the ritualized behaviors of organized religion alone. Rumi urges us not just to remain sober scholars of God, but to become rowdy lovers of God. He urges us to surrender to the powerful feelings of ecstatic love, which live in the middle of each and every body, just waiting for permission to be expressed. He wants us to know that it's okay to feel these energies and, even more, to surrender to them and be transformed by them—even if (*especially* if) they start making us feel as though we're getting spinny drunk and are losing our minds. In this state of intoxicated reverie, love takes over and shows us the way beyond our self.

Rumi's is a path for anyone who has ever felt the religious impulse but was never able to tame his or her energies to comfortably conform to the traditional religious model of composed tranquility. Rumi doesn't want you to remain calm and tranquil. He wants you to come alive, explode open, and become over-the-top drunk on the divine energies that live inside you.

Rumi's transformation from an orthodox religious teacher into an ecstatic lover of God came about through his chance encounter with a wandering dervish named Shams of Tabriz. The two men met in the streets of Konya. Something altogether extraordinary must have transpired between them in that moment of meeting, because they immediately went off together into a retreat room from which they didn't emerge for several months. When they did finally come back out into the world, they were in a highly illuminated state of sheer ecstatic wonderment. How could this have happened?!

What actually occurred behind the closed door of

their retreat room has been the subject of much debate, but a careful reading of the poetry that started pouring from Rumi's mouth strongly suggests that they were exploring the spiritual exercises and practices presented in this book. It's not enough simply to sit and talk about wanting to merge with the energies of God; one has to explore techniques and practices that allow this surrendered merging to actually occur.

After his encounter with Shams, Rumi entered a period during which he began to speak in the language of poetry as he moved and danced through Konya's streets, conversing with townspeople that he met along the way. He was always accompanied by an inner circle of students and friends who became known as the Secretaries of the Scribe and whose job was to write down the words that kept pouring from their teacher's mouth. After Rumi's death, the poems were compiled into twenty-three separate volumes, comprising some forty-four thousand verses and known collectively as the *Divan*.

While we owe the compilers a colossal debt of gratitude for preserving Rumi's words, their decision to group poems together not in chronological order, but according to things like similarities in poetic meter, makes the task of deciphering what Rumi was actually telling us all the more challenging (and causes utter consternation for the art historian, who relies on linear chronology to make sense of an artist's life work).

To put it impolitely, the *Divan* is a sprawling mess, but what a divine mess it is! Sometimes a poem seems to start and trail off, but then, several volumes later, you come across a passage that strikes you as far more thematically linked to the earlier poem than to anything in its near vicinity. Confounding things further, the numbered "poems" in each volume often read more like journal entries than they do discrete poems. An individual entry might include fragments from several conversations that Rumi had as he passed through the streets of Konya on a particular day. Each of the poems is a small puzzle in itself—deceptively simple, yet hinting at meanings that can spark long conversations. Because Rumi was a kind of trickster teacher, preferring to give out instructions through poetic clues that you have to figure out for yourself, the *Divan*'s jigsaw-puzzle nature is probably entirely appropriate.

Rumi spoke his poems spontaneously to people he met on his walks through the city; he didn't write them for readers to ponder over later. As much as possible, I've attempted to use wording to sound as though someone is speaking directly to you. On occasion, I've linked passages together that seem to complement and even complete each other. And I've altered some of the English phrases that are commonly used in translations of Sufi poetry to give readers unfamiliar with Sufi terminology a clearer sense of what I believe Rumi was pointing to. The more common *annihilation*, for example, becomes *melting down* or *melting away;* the *land of absence* becomes the *place where I disappear to.*

Mostly we think of spiritual practices and meditations as something we do with our minds, but all the practices that Rumi mentions—eating lightly, breathing deeply, moving freely, gazing raptly—are remarkably body oriented. His message is clear: if you want to change the psychology, you need to alter the physiology first. As a young man, Rumi had been taught the principle of *ma'iyya* by his father, who was an accomplished mystic in his own right. *Ma'iyya* tells us that God (or whatever word works for you) cannot be found in the mind alone (Buddhists, take note), cannot be found in the heart alone (a shocking belief for a Sufi to have), but needs to be *felt* everywhere in the body. Minute tactile sensations can be felt in every part of the body, down to the smallest cell, but ordinarily we don't let ourselves feel them. All too often, we hold the body still and suppress sensations, but then we're puzzled as to why we feel so numb and cut off from life. Love is not just an isolated affair of the heart alone, but of the whole body felt and accepted. Every little part of the body that we hold ourselves back from feeling is a part of love that we cut ourselves off from.

Each of the four practices presented here supports the awakening of soul through the stimulation of feeling, but the practices don't just affect the body; they also radically affect the mind by softening the hardened sense of self with which, ordinarily, we so completely identify:

Introduction

dissolving the self
is the creed and religion of lovers

there's no way to find your essence
without giving up your self

so melt yourself down
go to the place where you disappear completely
become nothing

look and see
I've seen everything in nothing

We all have a sense of individual self, a feeling that *I* exist as an individual entity, separate from everyone else and from everything else as well. We nurture, defend, and protect this self (and the body it lives and dies in) with every available resource—yet Rumi urges us to let it go, to dissolve it, to find out what lies beyond it.

Introduction

The problem with the self is that it inevitably bifurcates the world into *me* and *everything else,* and ecstatic love can only be found in moments of merging. The self lives in a world of separation, but the soul thrives on union. The self speaks through the monologue of silent thoughts that pass continuously through your mind, so Rumi speaks of the need for silence and for going to a place beyond words. The self can be felt as a contraction in the middle of your head, and so Rumi speaks of dissolving and softening it. When the self starts melting away, ordinary boundaries start melting along with it. When your self subsides, you feel intimately commingled with your world, no longer separate from it.

What might possibly lie beyond the self, and what is the state of union about which Rumi speaks so glowingly? No one can answer these questions for you. You have to find out for yourself, and that's where the practices in this book can help you. Each section begins with an introductory essay about the practice, followed by a selection of Rumi's poetry that speaks of it. Some of the poems read like literal instructions for the practice, while others allude to it more indirectly through metaphor and story. Many of the poems are funny, if not downright quirky; others go straight to the heart. This is not just another collection of beautiful Rumi poems to *ooh* and *ahh* over, however. It's a call to practice, an invitation to actually do something. As Rumi has said—referring to religious scripture (and, for that matter, to his own poems as well):

you can't untie this knot by listening to fairy tales
you have to do something inside yourself

So look upon each of these practices as an invitation to ecstasy, and know that your name is on the guest list. To gain entrance into ecstasy's party, all you need to do is to commit to doing practices that let you open to love's outrageous presence and pass beyond your self. What might this party be like? (Hint: it's no ordinary bar scene.) Listen to how Rumi describes what goes on there:

Introduction

o hearts gone wild
overcome by pleasure
ask for wine from the player
and surrender to the sound of the ney*

o sober ones
drink this wine from the jar of union,
then destroy the mind
that looks so far ahead of itself

open the ear of your soul,
listen to the music
at the tavern of eternity,
stop repeating the alphabet

for god's sake
fill your skull with that divine wine

---

*A ney is an ancient end-blown flute that figures prominently in Turkish, Persian, and Arabic music.

Introduction

and roll up the covers
of reason and the mind

o lovers
take off the garment of self-consciousness
and melt yourself away
while gazing at the face of immortal beauty

EATING LIGHTLY

From its range of tastes, smells, and the flavors that ensue, to its ability to transform the discomforting signals of hunger into sensations of satiety, food gives us pleasure. The preparation of food, the sharing of it with others, the sitting down to eat it—all of it gives us pleasure. After all, we don't eat and drink to be sad; we eat and drink to be merry, and so whenever humans gather together to celebrate, they most often do so around a table of delicious and carefully prepared food and drink.

Food gives us pleasure, but it also gives us problems. In the cultures of scarcity there's never enough, and in the cultures of abundance there's often too much. Too much can be as problematic as too little (although it must sound offensive to people who have too little to hear of the "problems" of having too much). Because our ancestors were never certain that the cache of berries and nuts that they so fortuitously discovered today would be found tomorrow, they would eat as much food as possible whenever they came across it, and all too often, under radically different conditions, we still enjoy doing fundamentally the same thing. Traits that long ago guaranteed our survival now contribute, in the cultures of too much, to an epidemic of overeating and its long list of serious health problems—as well as ensuring a life of despair in the cultures of too little.

Rumi would never tell us to forgo the pleasure of the food we eat, but he adds another twist to the connection between food and pleasure, one that compels us to reexamine our entire relationship with food and is especially pertinent in a world in which most people have either too little or too much available food. Beyond the pleasure of the chocolate in the mouth (and yes, it *is* pleasurable), there's an even greater pleasure to be found, Rumi tells us, and that pleasure arises through fasting.

For millennia many of our most prominent figures

have voluntarily given up eating food for a period ranging from a single day to fifty days and more, and they did so for the spiritual, physical, and mental benefits that fasting in the proper way and under the proper circumstances can uniquely provide. Fasting played an important role in the spiritual journeys of such diverse individuals as Moses, Buddha, Jesus, Mohammed, and Gandhi. Healers of the body—such as Hippocrates, Galen, Avicenna, and Paracelsus—embraced it for its ability to cure physical illness. The philosophers Socrates and Plato recommended fasting to their students and to members of the Academy because of its ability to increase mental clarity and to enhance physical functioning.

Billions of people on the planet today fast as part of religious ritual. Muslims eat no food during the days of Ramadan. Jews refrain from eating over Yom Kippur. Christians observe Lent. Native Americans fast as part of vision quests. Hindus and Buddhists each honor special days in their religious calendars by taking no food. And there are many more who fast on their own—not out of any religious observance, but simply because they enjoy how fasting makes them feel physically, emotionally, mentally, and even spiritually.

As a Muslim born to a devout family, Rumi grew up within a culture of fasting and would have participated fully in the observances of Islam's holy days. As he matured, he came to realize that fasting, while often initially entered into as an act of religious penance, was ultimately a practice of healing—not only of the body and mind, but of the soul itself. Eating large amounts of food feeds the you in you, but eating very little food feeds the god in you. Feasting has its place, but continual overeating adds fat to the very self that you hope to melt away. Fasting helps dissolve that self by stimulating the energies of ecstasy. During fasting, the sensations of the body start humming and vibrating again, and the mind eventually slows down and becomes quieter. Rumi always tells us to go inside and experience who we truly are, and periodic fasting was one of the fundamental tools he recommended for shining light onto our interior.

Fasting can be as simple as drinking water or juice for a day, or it can go on for weeks on end. If you've never fasted before, you'll want to speak to a health professional to make sure that you don't have any medical conditions or circumstances (diabetes or pregnancy, for example) that would prevent you from fasting. But if you're a candidate for fasting (and most reasonably healthy people are), let Rumi's words reassure and support you as you experiment with eating so lightly.

An enormous amount of information about fasting is available over the Internet and at book stores and libraries. You will find a huge variety of different kinds of fasts lasting for different lengths of time. Choose the fast that you intuitively resonate with and follow its instructions. If you're brand-new to fasting, start slowly with a short fast. And remember: not all of the time spent fasting will be pleasant because, on their journey out of your body, accumulated toxins can be released from deep within your cells. But the release of this ache and pain can help heal your body, settle your mind, and show you the mysteries your soul craves.

The Zulus have a saying: "The continually stuffed body can't see the secret things." Fasting, Rumi tells us, provides the kind of food that helps us see the mysteries and secret things in a way that the food of the table can't. So, when grappling with the issue of whether or not you should fast periodically, ask yourself the following question: is the pleasure of a well-fed belly enough for me, or do I also want to taste the ecstasy that Rumi speaks of as an even greater pleasure?

every year they dredge the canal
and clean the mud
so that water can flow
and green crops can grow again

if you give the bread of fasting
to the one who cleans and opens the canal
the fountain of life begins to flow
and the body's sensations come alive again

we've cleaned our heart and soul with fasting
the dirt that's been with us
has been washed away now

fasting causes some inevitable stress
but the invisible treasure of the heart gets revealed

fasting is wine for the soul
and gets you very drunk

Eating Lightly

you've seen what happens when you eat and drink
let's see what happens if you fast instead

fasting will make your neck thinner
but save you from death;
food and drink make your stomach full
but fasting makes you drunk;
quick, squeeze your waist
put on the belt of fasting;
try to obtain the eyes that see god
with the eyesight of fasting;
if you keep swimming for thirty days
back and forth in fasting's sea
in the end, my friend
you can't help but find its pearl

o shams of tebriz
you're drunkenness and sobriety both
you're the festival with sweet candies
and at the same time
the dignity, power, and honor of fasting

Eating Lightly

one by one
messengers came from the kitchen
saying angels have cooked halva in the sky

when the body eats halva
it goes to the bathroom
but when the soul eats halva
it flies to the sky

fasting makes you dizzy
lose weight
and become pale

but this loss of weight and color
will give you the white hands of moses*

---

*In Exodus 4:6, God instructs Moses to place his hand on his breast, and it immediately turns white in color.

Eating Lightly

yesterday you filled your stomach
with all kinds of bread and foods

you became so sluggish
so sleepy

what comes of such indulgence?
either recklessness
or the need to go to the toilet

sounds of moans and mourning
come from the soul while fasting
but the only sound that comes after a meal
is a low-pitched rumble from the rear end

so friend
if you want to hear what the soul has to say
then skip the meal;
if you want to hear from the other end
then bring the bowl closer to you

Eating Lightly

with the help of love's bread and water
men and women turn their faces
away from the wall of grief
and lose their appetite
for the bread and water of the table

drink the wine of eternity
give up eating and drinking
be full without food

at times we fill our belly
with the sun and the moon

at times we eat the clouds
without a belly
like the sun

the month of fasting is here
the table of soul has been set
we take our hands away from food

since fasting became our practice
soul's come alive again

since soul comes as a guest
let's keep offering our body

love is what I eat
it goes down well
and gives pleasure to my mouth

I eat a little bit of bread soaked in gravy
and used to eat a little trotter as well
but eating trotter
made me feel unwell

so from now on
I won't have anything to do with trotter
nor with anyone who's overly fond
of the meal and the table

eating
drinking
and a warm loaf of bread
are the lot of cold people

joy
ecstasy
and radiance
are the food of lovers

when you're fasting with your friends
you can still drink love's wine

the drunkenness from that wine
is completely different
from the drunkenness that causes you shame
and makes you sneak home like a scorpion

so keep on drinking the cupless, jarless wine
that doesn't break your fast

just know that it doesn't come
from grapes, wheat, or barley

if you constantly throw stones
with the catapult of fasting
the castle of darkness
comes tumbling down

keep throwing stones with the catapult of fasting
at the fortress of disbelief
the towers of darkness

most people live in the world
of donkeys and oxen

they crawl toward love

if you were truly a lover
you wouldn't eat like that

immersed in darkness
because of eating and drinking
your shirt becomes stained
with the sweat of self

if you take fasting to heart

you'll hear the sound

I am at your service

I am at your service

every time you call out

my god

Eating Lightly

my heart wants the halva
that brings peace and pleasure to the sufi
and what a delicious halva it is!
its smell rises up from the top
in every breath I take

you eat this halva
with your heart
without touching your hand to your mouth
just like a fig
whose mouth remains closed

this halva comes from the other world

so eat there
without your hands
without your mouth

Eating Lightly

time to celebrate!
the month of fasting is here

I wish a good journey
to everyone who keeps company
with those who are fasting

I climbed the roof
to see the moon,
the lord of fasting got me so drunk!

I lost my hat
while gazing at the moon
and then I lost my mind

there's another secret moon besides this one,
it's hiding out in the tent of fasting

so anyone who comes this month
to the harvest of fasting
finds the way to this moon

I'm a doctor,
and I want you to go on a diet

fear has made you sick
and caused you to lose hope

stay on this diet
and I'll make a potion for you

when you drink it
you'll never come back to yourself

the month of fasting has come
so let's not talk about the bowl or jar

from now on
let's enjoy the pitcher of eternity
and get drunk
off of that pitcher

when you're fasting
you're the guest of god
and are served the meal of heaven

when you shut the door of hell this month
thousands of heaven's gates spring open

A certain youth in the service of a great king was dissatisfied with the amount of food he was being given, so he went to the cook and scolded him:

"By the stinginess of your portions, you dishonor our master!"

The youth wouldn't listen to the cook's excuses but wrote off an angry letter of complaint and sent it to the king. The letter was outwardly complimentary and respectful, but it betrayed an angry spirit.

On receiving this letter, the king saw that it contained only complaints about meat and drink and showed no aspirations for spiritual food. Therefore, he decided it needed no answer, as "the proper answer to a fool is silence."

When the youth received no answer to his letter, he was much surprised and threw the blame on the cook and on the messenger, ignoring the fact that the folly of his own letter was the real reason for its having gone unanswered.

He wrote the king five letters, but the king persisted in his refusal to reply, saying that fools are enemies of God and man and that he who has any dealings with a fool just ends up fouling his own nest. Fools only regard material meat and drink, whereas the food of the wise is the light of God. Fasting is the food of God, the means by which spiritual food is obtained.

One day some travelers from another land begged the Prophet for food and lodging. The Prophet was moved by their entreaties and instructed each of his disciples to take one of the strangers to his home and feed and lodge him there. So each disciple selected one of the strangers and invited him back to his home as a guest.

But there was one big and coarse man, a veritable giant, whom no one would receive, and so the Prophet took him back to his own home. In his compound, the Prophet had seven she-goats to supply his family with milk, and the hungry stranger devoured all the milk of the seven goats (to say nothing of all the bread and meats!) and left not a drop for the Prophet's family. Understandably, the family was very annoyed—so annoyed in fact that, when the stranger retired to his chamber for the night, one of the maidservants locked him in.

During the night, the stranger began to feel unwell because of having eaten so much. He got up from his bed and tried to get out into the open air, but he was unable to do so because of the locked door. Finally, he became very sick and defiled his bedding.

In the morning, he was extremely ashamed, and the moment the door was opened, he ran away. The Prophet was aware of what had happened but let the man escape so as not to cause him further shame. After he had gone, the servants saw the mess he had made and informed the Prophet of it, but the Prophet made light of it and said he would clean it up himself.

While the Prophet was engaged in this work, the stranger came back to look for a talisman he'd left behind in his hurry to escape. As soon as he saw what the Prophet was doing, he burst into tears and apologized profusely for his filthy conduct. But the Prophet consoled him, saying that his weeping and penitence would purge the offense, and explained how the outward acts of prayer and fasting bear witness to the spiritual light within.

After being nurtured on this spiritual food, the stranger renounced his gluttony. He thanked the Prophet for bringing him to the knowledge of the true faith and bringing him back to life. The Prophet was satisfied with his sincerity and asked him to sup with him again.

At supper, the stranger drank only half a portion of milk yielded by one goat and steadfastly refused to take any more, saying he felt perfectly satisfied with the little he had already taken. The other guests marveled at how the stranger's gluttony had been cured so soon and reflected on the virtues of the spiritual food that the Prophet had served.

BREATHING DEEPLY

The most important food our body needs is the oxygen in the air we breathe. We can live without solid food for months on end and go without water for days, but if oxygen is taken away from us for even a few minutes, our body dies, and we move on to whatever awaits us next.

As critical as oxygen is for our survival, however, most of us suppress our breath and breathe with only a fraction of the capacity actually available to our lungs, and we do this by holding our body still. Each of us has developed a signature holding pattern in the tissues of the body, a unique way in which we tense individual muscles and fascia in order to contain and hold back on the power of the breath. But, in holding back on the breath, we hold back on ourselves.

In order to accommodate the full power of the breath, the entire body needs to be very supple and relaxed. Have you ever watched how a sleeping baby breathes? The movements of breath can be seen passing through its entire body in a beautifully fluid, wavelike motion. The movements in the head look like tidal waters, which quickly ebb and flow; the little body expands . . . and contracts with movements of human grace and fluidity that you're unlikely to see anywhere else. Over time, though, as we grow and age, we follow the example of our elders (who followed the example of theirs) and learn how to contain the breath by bringing tension into our body so that this once natural wave of resilient motion no longer occurs. It's as though the waters in our body start to freeze and can no longer allow the motion of breath to pass effortlessly through.

But what are we holding back on? And what are we so afraid of surrendering to? The power of the breath is a very potent force, and it wants to breathe us. What might happen if we were to surrender to this most natural of forces instead of holding back on it?

Like so many other spiritual teachers before and since, Rumi was keenly aware of the integral connection between how we breathe and our condition of mind. While our diminished patterns of breath are still adequate to ensure the continued life of our physical body, they're not adequate to nurture the ecstatic life of our soul. A cultural pattern of holding that inhibits the breath comes with a high price tag. When we don't breathe freely, our vitality suffers, we gradually lose touch with the shimmering nature of bodily sensation, and we often end up trapped in the chatter of our minds. But if we're able to relax, soften, and free up the restrictions to our breathing so we can start surrendering to each and every breath, allowing it to breathe us however it wants—our body becomes energized, tactile sensations come out of hiding, and the involuntary monologue of the mind stands a chance of becoming still. As the chatter of mind quiets down, the energies and sensations of soul start coming out to play.

Breath can bind you or free you; it all depends on how much conscious attention you bring to it. If you bring none, breath will still go on automatically, but it will almost certainly be contained. Because you can remedy this automatic tendency to suppress the breath by consciously attending to it, and because doing so possesses such a powerful capacity to affect consciousness, spiritual teachers of all ages have used techniques of breathing as tools for spiritual awakening. Common to all of the many diverse schools of Buddhism is the practitioner's observation of, gradual surrender to, and eventual merging with the breath. Taoist masters employed breath techniques to alter consciousness and prolong physical longevity. The Indian science and art of *pranayama,* which focuses solely on different breathing exercises, has always been an essential part of a yogi's practices. And then there are the powerful contemporary breath therapies such as Rebirthing and Holotropic Breathwork, which stem in part from the seminal work of Wilhelm Reich, the first Western psychotherapist to recognize the power of the breath in the therapeutic process.

Every one of these techniques is powerfully effective, and yet they're all very different. In some you may be instructed to take long, slow breaths; in others you breathe in rapid staccato bursts. Some instruct you to breathe through your nose, while others tell you to breathe through the mouth—and even others tell you to do both. Some tell you to hold the breath for a certain number of counts during the pauses between inhalation and exhalation; others tell you to avoid the pauses altogether. What these techniques all share and hold deeply in common, however, is their understanding that paying conscious attention to the breath, learning how to explore and tap its power, is an extremely effective way to grow in soul.

In some of his poems, Rumi sounds like a yogi recommending the practice of deep-belly breathing and a prolonged *kumbaka,* the holding of the breath, and there are still Sufi schools today that practice the retention of breath as a spiritual discipline:

god's free creatures
touched by his wine and wind
fill their bellies with their breath
hold it deep
and keep silent

In other poems, Rumi sounds more like a classical Buddhist, reminding us not to let our minds wander off:

with every breath you take
remember:
keep the mind in the middle of the head

And in others still, he draws on shared Jewish, Christian, and Muslim beliefs by linking our connection with God to every breath:

if you want to protect your heart
then remember god
in every breath you take

Of all the many references to the breath that occur in Rumi's poetry, however, and of all the many pithy instructions on breath that Rumi gives, none is mentioned more often than *the breath of love.* Sometimes Rumi will also speak of this quality of breath as *the breath of Jesus,* because he viewed the historical Jesus as a great teacher of love. For Rumi, love was at once both the source and the goal of all spiritual unfolding:

wherever you are
in whatever circumstances you find yourself
strive to be a lover

Love is the force of attraction that draws us to complete ourselves through union with another. Sometimes this other takes the form of another person, and we rightly speak of this friend as our personal beloved. But Rumi suggests that we also want to consummate our love with the larger energies of the soul—which we feel pressing out from inside us, wanting to burst forth and express themselves—and he referred to this internal courtship as the love affair with the universal Beloved. Rumi viewed these energies as a palpable force of such magnitude that, once you became aware of them, the only sane response would be to submit to them—and, if they tore you apart in the process, so be it. But conventional wisdom views things differently, and so we hold back on these energies and contain the breath, but then are left wondering why love seems so elusive.

To understand what a breath of love might be like, and how we might practice this breath, first imagine for a moment what its opposite, a breath of fear, would be like. Fear comes in many forms, but it always involves some degree of holding still and some degree of resistance. The classic mime's expression of sudden fright is a sharp, startled inhalation and, at the very top of the inhalation, the sudden freezing of the whole body. In contrast, a breath of love would be relaxed and fluid with inhalations and exhalations melting smoothly from one into the next. And the body too would have to be relaxed and malleable, able to let the breath billow and blossom and then subside and pass through its entire length with minimal interference or resistance.

Love always begins by loving and accepting yourself, and not at all surprisingly, this act of self-acceptance leads directly to the energies of the Beloved. Most of the time, we don't let ourselves feel the full range of sensations that pass through our body. In fact, we hold back from feeling them by doing exactly what we do to resist the breath: we bring tension into the body and hold it still. To practice directing love to yourself, wouldn't it make sense to start opening to the feeling of these bodily sensations and energies every time you breathe? The Beloved can be met and pursued in the deep energies of the body and in the breath that allows you to feel these energies.

So one possible way you might practice a breath of love would be:

Breathing Deeply

As you breathe in, breathe into the felt awareness of your entire body. As you breathe out, feel your whole body exhaling.

As you breathe in, let yourself feel every single cell in your body.

As you breathe out, let yourself dissolve and merge into the outer world.

Feel your gratitude for being alive, for having life given to you so freely each and every moment in the air you breathe. Gratitude toward the world is the natural feeling state of someone in love.

And, finally, see if you can relax even further into the breath by allowing subtle movement to occur between each and every vertebra of the spine every time you inhale and exhale. As you breathe in, the spine lengthens effortlessly along its curves; as you breathe out, it rocks back down.

Love can be found through the release of holding. Allowing the force of breath—each and every breath—to breathe through you however it wants to is to submit to love.

The state of embodied grace, which Rumi says can be ours if we want it, is not some kind of condition that you evolve into and then rest in for the remainder of your life. It needs to be earned in each and every breath you take. This one . . . and then this one . . . and now this one . . . Bringing a practice of breath awareness into your life is Rumi's second recommendation for drawing ecstasy closer.

lovers o lovers

wake up

it's time to leave this world!

I can hear the sound of the exit drums

with the ear of my soul

here, right now,

the caravan master

sets the string of camels

and asks his fee;

why have you slept all this time

o people of the caravan?

the sounds of the bells

on the necks of the camels

are the call of departure

come

let's travel to the land of soul and breath

the land where we disappear

bringing breath to life
is the essence of every religion
and the remedy for every illness

let every breath you take
cleanse the soul of its grief and pain
so it can keep glowing brightly inside you

when the lover breathes
flames spread through the universe

a single breath shatters this world of illusion
into the tiniest particles

the world becomes an ocean
from beginning to end
and then the ocean disappears into rapture

at that moment the sky splits open
an uproar fills the world
and all time, space, and existence disappear

before we ever met you
we couldn't really breathe
because time had choked us

from now on we'll be slaves
to the breath of love

run away to god
he's the fountain of life

find his blessing
in every breath you take

now is the time to be silent

don't even try to describe
the water and pearl in his ocean

if you really want to dive into that sea
then hold your breath
hold your breath

everyone worships your love
the universe is in your hand

in one breath
we become drunk in your temple

in another breath
we fall into your dreaminess

open your chest
to the early morning breeze
so death can come back to life
and these old tired bones
can start feeling fresh again

the breath of love calls out
from the very center of existence:
in every moment
come back to life

one kind of breath
rises up in love

one kind of breath
falls down with joy

one kind of breath
embraces the beloved

and one kind of breath
makes gossip and starts wars

Breathing Deeply

beloved friend,
you're even finer
than the breath that comes
from early dawn's breeze

you're such a breath
that god said
you could bring the dead
back to life

god actually said that about you!

so blow your breath into me
and inflate me like a bag
I'll float on top of the sea

there's not a single day
that you don't blow like that
and if there ever was such a day
not a single blade of grass would grow
on the plains or in the valleys

I'm not going to wait around
for the sound of death's trumpet
to bring me back to life

love gives me new life
in every moment
in every breath

where is jesus
whose breath is so holy and overflowing
that even if he'd never been born
he would still be revered?

even though you can't see him with your eyes
you can still feel his breathing

learn how to touch soul
in every breath you take
and watch yourself
turn into the messiah

when your soul is cleansed
in every breath you take
you'll understand
how to give birth to jesus
every time you breathe

there's a new garden
a new meadow in our soul
there's a new story
a new legend in our ear
in every breath we take

you serve a different wine at your tavern

it brings a different joy and pleasure
to every particle of my body

in this breath
you bring death back to life

in this breath
you offer a brand new glass

in this breath
a bottle of wine's coming toward me

in this breath
I drink a glass of eternity

we're engulfed by soul's sea
in every breath we take

if that's not so
then why do these waves keep coming
one after the other
from the ocean of heart?

the smell of the beloved
is on my breath

there are gardens
meadows
and jasmine

your breath is food
for the brides of the garden

if that breath became dirt in my body
I'd grow love's roses
from head to foot

Breathing Deeply

we may be human beings
but we're strangers to the breath

we have to burn the self
inside us to ashes

only then
will we know the breath

the waters of immortality's fountain
can be found in the breath in your lungs

we get drunk on every breath
from the wine that has no origin

this wine must be hundreds of years old!

if I serve it in every breath
in my strange condition of mind . . .
I wonder what will happen to me

a mansion in the sky
can be yours with each breath
yet all too often
what you do instead
is fall into dreams or doubt

so offer wine every moment
every breath

and remember:

every breath you take
makes one of two choices:
you either surrender to your soul
or struggle with doubt

if you're really not aware
that god is constantly hunting for you
then pay close attention
to every breath you take

the helpless ney can't make a sound
without the breath of the one who blows it

go to the cemetery
see all those broken neys

the breath of the ney players has ceased
there's no life
no talk left

their voices say silently
we and I are all gone from us

MOVING FREELY

Ecstasy moves. It never stands still. It can be thought of as an ex-stasis, a leaving behind of whatever's been holding us still and an emerging or coming out from the cocoon that stillness has woven. When we're able to move freely and surrender to the larger forces of breath and feeling energies that want to pass through our body, palpable feelings and expressions of ecstasy naturally start materializing.

But just as we breathe with only a fraction of the capacity available to our lungs, so do we mostly move through only a fraction of the range of motion available to our joints. Holding the body still can only occur in an environment that values control over ecstasy. The wheels of commerce often move through still bodies, and so, to make our way in the world, we often inhibit our breath, stifle our awareness of sensations, and resist the impulse to move. But when we get home at night, it's time to let our hair down, turn the music up, and let the body awaken.

The impulse to move is as old as life itself. Viewed under a microscope, the single cells of the most primitive life forms can be seen to swell, contract, gyrate, bulge, suck in, puff out, spin, and glide as they move along their way. Life moves. Life doesn't want to stand still, and so, as the earliest humans surrendered to their primal impulse to move, the activity of dance began to emerge as one of the first ritualized forms of human behavior.

Rumi may have started out an orthodox cleric, but he became an ecstatic dancer. Through his understanding of breath and fasting, and propelled by his explosive meeting and communion with Shams of Tabriz, strong energies of soul must have been awakened in his body. Like so many others before and since, Rumi discovered that the pressures of these strong feeling energies—which Sufis describe as the intense and awakened longing in the heart and soul for union with whatever they feel so achingly separate from—could be relieved and released through surrendering to the movements of the dance. Some people believe that Shams introduced Rumi to the dance during their retreat, while others have suggested that Rumi opened to it himself after Shams had left when, out of despair over the loss of his great friend, he began turning round and around a pillar and didn't want to stop. Either way, the encounter with Shams was the catalyst that helped Rumi awaken dormant feeling energies and sensations, and a natural response to this kind of awakening is to start dancing. Musicians became Rumi's highly valued friends, fueling the dance that kept his body in motion and freeing the poetic language in which he began to speak as he moved about town.

Dance became, for Rumi, a form of physical prayer that helps to loosen the tight grip of the self and to experience the energies of ecstasy, and so he began inviting friends to come together as a group and perform a ceremony of dance and music that he called the *sema*. After his death, Rumi's son Sultan Veled would preserve his father's teachings by founding the Mevlevi Order, which continues to this day to perform *sema* and to train people in what has come to be known as the dance of the whirling dervish.

We dance for many reasons—some personal, some social—but the dance's ability to open the dancer to altered feeling and visionary states is as old as human life. We're currently living at a time in which the power of the dance is experiencing an emergence on a scale that has never been seen before, and the simple explanation for this is that music has become so ubiquitous. Music has always been an instigator of the dance, but for the better part of recorded history, music was a sublime rarity. We've now learned how to literally record history, and the sounds of music are being transmitted everywhere. A good band in a groove catalyzes the dance like nothing else, and the music that's being listened to the most around the planet has a sound and a beat that bodies want to move to. Over the past fifty years, improvisational dance, as a form of personal healing and spiritual practice, has exploded from the pioneering teaching of people like Bapak Subuh, Gabrielle Roth, and Emilie Conrad into the planetary rave movement, which has turned millions of people into ecstatic dancers. *Liberate the dancer within* has become a spiritual motto for increasingly large numbers of young people everywhere on the planet. Liberating the dancer within (and, yes, we all, every single one of us, have a dancer inside us wanting to move) is Rumi's third essential practice for sparking ecstasy.

Many of Rumi's poems, read as invitations to simply surrender to the felt urgency to move, sound like teachings from the improvisational dance movement. How does one learn to dance? Just listen to the music, and let your body move. Still not sure? Look at how the branches on the trees move in a wind. They don't try to do this step or that step. They just surrender to the breeze that moves them. Move like that, Rumi tells us. Move like the dust particles dancing in the light. Just surrender to the movement that wants to move you.

Others of Rumi's poems speak specifically of the highly ritualized practice of turning the body in circles—round and around, over and over again, with arms outstretched. While the formal rituals of turning have been preserved in the *sema* ceremony of the Mevlevi Order, the actions of whirling, turning, and spinning around are universal to everyone (and, the Sufis would say, to everything). Little children love to spin around, and they're always filled with giddy joy when they do. Because turning can make you dizzy, you have to find a way to go beyond your mind, and this place beyond is ecstasy's playground. While anybody can explore the turn on their own (the basic directions for turning couldn't be simpler: stand with arms outstretched, the right palm facing up, the left palm facing down; keep your gaze fixed on the back of your left hand, and begin to turn to your left round and around in circles— and then surrender to whatever starts happening to you. . . .), people who feel particularly drawn to this unique form of ecstatic prayer may want to seek out teachers and communities for deeper guidance and training.

Music, Rumi tells us, is food for lovers. Wherever music is, dance follows, and music is now everywhere. So let the poems that follow inspire you to bring a dance practice into your life. Turn the lights down.

Turn your music system on, and play whatever music is drawing you right now. And then let your body start to move. Don't force it to do this or that. Just let it start to awaken, and follow its lead. The ecstasy is in finding out how it wants to move you and where it wants to take you.

Moving Freely

if you're smart
and want to grow in soul
you'll give thanks to our king
and keep dancing

o sufis
keep whirling and dancing

for god's sake
go ecstatic!

put the belt of rapture
around your waists
and start doing sema

Moving Freely

my beautiful moon is dancing
venus plays the tambourine

I salute the brave
who proclaim their love
through dance and music

you start out imitating
end up terrified
and then find hope

start dancing with that hope

in time you'll break free
from this world of illusion

bats in the night sky
love dancing with darkness

birds that love the sun
dance from dawn to dusk

o fast-blowing morning breeze
go and tell shams of tebriz:
tell me who you are
and come dance with me

Moving Freely

you're so beautiful
heart and soul fell in love
and started dancing at your gathering

when they heard the angel gabriel
was coming down to earth
all the particles of the land
started dancing

the sun of his face conquered the moon
who was thrilled to be held in his arms
and started dancing

o my king
you grow in love
like a baby with its mother's smile

so come
let yourself go
get in the dance

after seeing him
you came speeding
like a ball to his bat
you lost your head
you lost your feet
so you danced
without your head or feet

you've gotten so drunk
on the wine of being
you've got ecstasy
written all over you

ecstasy keeps calling
so get ready for the journey

start to dance

Moving Freely

untie your hair
spread your scent around
put the souls of sufis to dancing

the sun, moon, and stars
keep turning around the sky;
we're in the middle
turning around the center

your singing and playing
are so beautiful!
even the lowest notes
start turning the sufis of the sky

the spring breeze comes running
singing
making the world smile

it causes a commotion
among the young

Moving Freely

every day a fairylike beauty
steps out from behind the curtain
and puts everyone in a circle to dance

the sufi dances to that beauty's tune
and waves his soft cloak

but the man of reason
gets confused

his turban comes untied
and drags on the ground

the stirring sound of his voice
comes from deep inside
the oven of his heart

when he starts spreading melodies
my heart jumps from its seat

he put a rebab* on his lap
took the cap off his head
and set it on the ground

when I saw his head
begin to shake
my heart went right to him

---

*A rebab is a stringed instrument.

Moving Freely

heart spins
his silk thread
like a bobbin

it turns so fast
that the spinner of the thread
sometimes sees it
sometimes doesn't

body is like dust and soil
soul is like the wind

soul kicks up the dust
and through the dance of particles
soul is revealed

so let's say your soul
looks a lot like dust and soil
and another soul
meets you in that dust

the whole universe
will start to dance
particle by particle
to your tune

come

come and see

that you are the soul of sema

come

come and see

that you're a walking cypress

in sema's garden

come and see

that someone exactly like you

has never existed before

and never will again

come and see

that the eyes of sema

have never seen anyone like you before

and never will again

what should I do
if love seizes me?

start dancing of course!

sweep love into your arms
and press her to your chest

when particles of dust
are touched by the sun
they spread their arms and start whirling
to a music no one can hear

a sweet voice came
from the threshold of greatness
come
it says to soul

how could soul resist?

how could a fish out of water lie still
with the sound of the waves in its ears?

the fish wants to jump back into the sea

how could a sufi not enter the dance
like a particle of dust under eternal light?

a bright light
shines in the sky
coming from the dance of lovers

yet still there are those
who condemn dance and music
and don't believe it's right

one group turns around the sun
and falls into god's favor

the other just keeps turning
around the cold harsh winter

when you hear the songs of birds
your wings begin to flutter

if you really want to fly
free your feet from the tar

look at these particles
in front of my window
they're dancing so exquisitely in the air

these particles dance sema
like sufis in the sun's light
but to what kind of music, beat, or instrument
nobody knows

the most important sema
is the one that goes on inside us

particles of our body are dancing
with hundreds of different rhythms and graces

those who've attained
open their arms and start dancing
at a place beyond truth or lies

they don't get involved
with matters of the head
or the soul

someone once offered a dervish
a totally bodiless soul
but the dervish just whispered
back in his ear
no thanks

Moving Freely

o my mind
I asked
where have you gone?

I turned into wine
he answered back
how can I behave
like a grape anymore?

burn your soul and put its ashes
on your eyes as a salve

blindness will disappear from the world

souls enter sema
and turn into honey bees

they swarm around the honey
that's never been tasted

we're moving and dancing
like a flag on your wind

I'm going to the place
where I disappear completely

the clouds cleared away from your face

the sky split apart into layers
and shone like moonlight
through all the windows

the light became stronger
it broke all the souls into pieces

souls started dancing
particle by particle
in front of the sun
flying around everywhere
saying
what will be will be

the dome of the sky keeps turning
but the skies of love whirl much faster

the whirling sky turns only for lovers
so get up and join in
let's start turning!

ours is the path
of joy and pleasure
music and dance
not stillness
not denial

the only one who benefits
from a pearl dropped on the road
is the one who takes the journey

the one who doesn't
turn around that pearl
will have nothing

spring has given
the call to prayer

get up and come to the garden!

listen for the voices
in the tulips and the mountain

learn how to dance
from the branches of the trees

Moving Freely

love keeps changing inside us
into so many different shapes and forms

every moment
a different feeling
wants to pass through your heart
but your body's become frozen
and turned into stone

until you understand
the patterns in your heart
you won't really be able to move

an amazing dance is going on
from the bottom of the earth
to the top of the sky

once you've become a stream of particles
don't go and become a mountain again

even the whirling sky
became jealous of our turning

because this is the real thing
the other's just a shell

this is the real light
the other's just a small fire

Moving Freely

my friend
it's time for sema
time to get up and jump

you've been asleep on a boat
for a thousand nights;
open your sail
and get up and jump

the heavy feeling in your head
made you sleep a long time
but they woke you up
so get up and jump

o flying thoughts
keep flying
keep jumping right through
this bewildered body!

Moving Freely

come to your senses
the sufi is the child of the moment
forget about last year and next year and jump

it pays to be generous
when doing business with god
because love weighs more
than the whole steel yard
get up and jump!

get up and jump
like the waves of the sea
roaring with love
because pearls are being spread at their feet

if you're feeling run-down
like straight, limp hair
parted in the middle
then jump up
like the springing curls in the hair of the beloved

for way too long
you've been lied to and bullied;
why don't you jump right out
of this mean old world?

I get involved too much in making rhymes
so shhhhh. . .
let's jump together
without any words this time

it doesn't matter
how the branch moves

as long as it moves
it means there's a breeze

o branch
don't think you have to move
this way or that way
and don't try to run away either

don't you know
that the only guidance you'll ever need
comes from the wind?

Moving Freely

one particle says to another:
how long are we going to fly in the air?

only your beautiful hand knows

weather changes
in hundreds of ways
from dawn to dusk;
in every shape it takes
it whirls and dances for you

even if you can't see the air moving
you can still watch the trees
and see the souls dancing around god

Moving Freely

we've learned our melodies
from the revolving spheres

the song of the spheres
is what we sing with our voice
and play on our strings

as we're all members
of the family of adam
we've all heard these melodies in paradise
and even though we're now covered
in earth and water
we still have faint memories
of those songs of heaven

but while we're covered up
in these earthly clothes
how can the tones of the dancing spheres reach us?

Moving Freely

and so it is
that listening to music is lovers' food
because it reminds them
of their union with god

even if your beloved turns into a fire
jump into it anyway and keep burning

burn up like a candle and melt

a divine dance appears in the soul and the body
at the time of peace and union

anyone can learn this dance

just listen to the music

Moving Freely

without your blessing
no one
not even the embryo inside the womb
would move

it's not just the movement
in the womb or in ecstasy

even the bones in the grave
dance with your radiance

we dance so much to the tunes of this world
come on friends
get ready for the dance in the other world

souls move around
with these rough coarse covers

Moving Freely

once they throw off those heavy covers
then watch how they dance!

before we were born
we kept kicking and moving
in the darkness of the womb
just to express our heartfelt thanks

we are all sufis
who came dancing from the dervish convent
to give thanks for these blessings

GAZING RAPTLY

You've purified the body through fasting and breath. You've opened to the movements of the dance. Now it's time to meet the friend.

Of the four practices that Rumi promotes in his poetry, none is mentioned so prominently and frequently as the simple action of sitting down across from a dear friend, looking into each other's eyes, holding each other's gaze, and surrendering to the radical alteration to body and self that naturally starts occurring. For centuries, Sufis have revered the relationship between Rumi and Shams as a kind of divine mystery that could only be marveled at, but never understood. No one knew for certain what went on behind the closed doors of their retreat room—what kind of interactions must have transpired between them to have sparked the intoxicated state of ecstasy they were in when they finally emerged from their retreat. But how could it have been missed? It's everywhere in the poetry! Melting into the gaze of one's friend is one of Rumi's greatest legacies and gifts to anyone who has ever felt the pull of the ecstatic and is trying to figure out how to give birth to it.

However, while I believe that what Rumi and Shams were doing together can no longer be considered a complete mystery, if you truly want to understand what happened to them, you'll need to experience it for yourself. To bring completely alive the story of Rumi and Shams' ecstatic dissolving into the shared consciousness of union, you'll want to do what they did. You'll want to seek out and find a friend and explore the practice for yourself.*

Something happens to two people who come together, look into each other's eyes, hold the gaze,

———

*For more on the gazing practice, which can open the door to a profoundly ecstatic state of divine union, please see my earlier book *The Spiritual Practices of Rumi: Radical Techniques for Beholding the Divine*. It is devoted solely to this particular practice.

and . . . surrender. Almost immediately you start feeling things . . . as if dormant sensations of the body and soul start waking up from a long slumber. The visual field may become altered, as hard edges soften and the shape of your partner's face shifts. You may laugh. You may cry. You may feel very scared and alone. You may feel overwhelmed with joy. Eventually, you may start feeling the energies in your heart and soul being drawn toward your friend as if by a strong magnet. Closer, ever closer, you feel your consciousness and energies starting to dance and commingle with your friend, until eventually you arrive at a place of such closeness and intimacy that you realize that you don't feel separate from your friend anymore—that your soul has merged with her soul and you can no longer tell the difference. This play of two ordinarily separate souls relaxing into a condition that is separate no longer is, for Rumi, what real friendship is all about.

But mostly we don't look at each other in this way. We resist surrendering to the compelling and natural desire for merging into union that wants to occur whenever two people lay eyes on each other. We're leery of going beyond the self even if ecstasy is the offered reward. We don't have time in our busy lives to allow an unraveling of our karmic knots by participating in a prolonged and surrendered gaze with a friend. How prolonged? Virtually everyone can get a taste of where this gazing is leading to in just a few minutes (indeed, one of the beauties of the mutual gaze is that its effects can be felt so immediately). The real depths that the practice can take you to, however, only start revealing themselves after long hours. Remember that Rumi and Shams spent long weeks and even months exploring what was happening to them. Connecting through the gaze sends both friends off on a journey of unfolding through the landscape of the soul; the longer you stay surrendered to the gaze, the more sights you get to see. The longer you spend in the gaze, the deeper you heal. Who, then, has time for the gaze? Babies do. Their parents do. Lovers do. And ecstatic friends do.

The first three practices can all be done alone. To explore the practice of gazing, you need to find a friend—someone whom you feel drawn to and who is drawn to you, someone who is as excited as you are to explore and play the great game of gazing and dissolving, someone who wants to risk being himself with another. You can gaze and go deep in this way with anyone, but in truth, over time you may find that you're especially drawn to gazing with a particular someone and she with you. The gaze with this person simply feels right and starts initiating journeys you've never been on before with anyone else. Maybe your life circumstances will allow you to go into retreat together and spend long days and weeks just as Rumi and Shams did. Maybe they won't. But know that you've found a friend, and explore the practice together as much as you can. Be forewarned, though. The practice is highly addictive to both body and soul, and you may want to spend a great deal of time together.

The basic instructions for the gaze are so simple. Sit or lie comfortably with your friend, and begin looking at each other. Look right into the eyes that are looking right back at you . . . and relax. What starts happening? Can you feel it? Can you accept the shifts that almost immediately start occurring in your awareness of body and self? Can you accept the unraveling of emotion and memory that begins to spread through you in waves of feeling? The more you relax into the gaze, the more you'll be able to accept whatever comes to you: strong sensations, unusual perceptions, emotions.

Over time, the body and the mind start losing their unrelenting sense of solidity and become more fluid and watery, like a river with a current running through it. The more you connect with the organic current of the gaze and are able simply to surrender to it, the deeper you go on your journey beyond the self. The current takes you here. It takes you there. Sometimes, the river is placid and beautiful. Other times, rapids appear out of nowhere. It doesn't matter. Just stay connected through the gaze, keep surrendering to the current, and accept whatever's around the next bend. Where does this river run to? If anyone knows, there would be no way to tell you. The only way you can find out is to jump in yourself, surrender to its current, and trust in its wisdom. Rumi and Shams must have surrendered completely, and the journey they took together is still rightly revered.

You can go on this journey too. If you already have a special friend in your life, start exploring the practice together. If you don't have that special friend but would like to, then prepare yourself for the meeting by exploring movement practices, fasting, and the power of the breath. The friend that you're wanting to meet is preparing himself as well. And keep your eyes open. You never know when you're going to meet the friend. For all you know, she may be right around the corner. And when you do meet, acknowledge your good fortune by surrendering to your friend's gaze as much as you're able. May the following poems from the master gazer inspire you to seek out a friend and discover for yourself what the extraordinary union of eye to eye is all about.

Gazing Raptly

my heart got caught
in his drunken eyes

now I'm drunk
and out of my mind

when you turn your face away
the water in the canal stops flowing

how can particles appear
if the sun doesn't shine on them?

Gazing Raptly

an image of a face
appeared before my eyes
and started speaking:

I've come from the garden of the beloved

by way of the back room of the tavern keeper

look into my dreamy eyes

I'm the drunkenness you crave

I'm high and low both

I've come like a whirling sky

from the very beginning of creation

I came to befriend the soul

and then to merge with it

I went back

but I returned again

like a compass making constant turns

around one point

Gazing Raptly

I asked him
are you here to help me?

he answered
that's the only reason I'm here
I'm the moon
you're my light

look into my eyes
get inside my eyes

I've chosen to live
in a different mansion
behind my eyes

my eyes
are a jar of wine

my eyelashes
are the wine filter

your face
is my faith

your gaze
is my religion

trust love

love is a face and eyes
turned this way
gazing at you

just face
just vision

if you've got the pearls
then come and gaze
into the ocean of my eyes

Gazing Raptly

o watermaster
start the fountain
wake up the garden
let the flowers open their eyes

your goodness is hidden
like the fountain of life
inside the darkness of your eyes

pupils like that
turn eyes into oceans

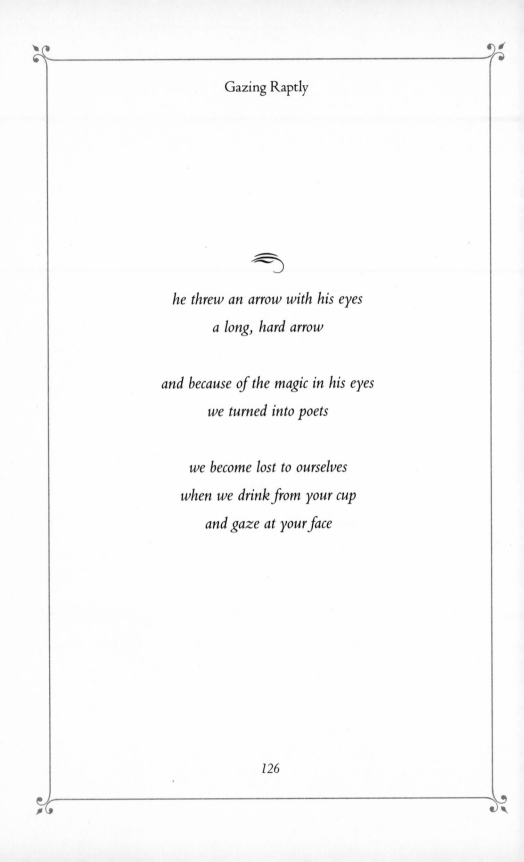

he threw an arrow with his eyes
a long, hard arrow

and because of the magic in his eyes
we turned into poets

we become lost to ourselves
when we drink from your cup
and gaze at your face

Gazing Raptly

when the fire in his eyes
melts into grace . . .

poison becomes honey
the wolf becomes the shepherd
mountains turn to mush

the bitter salty sea
turns into the fountain of life

holy light shines out
from his hidden face
to all people everywhere

and his soft, dreamy eyes
keep on looking at us

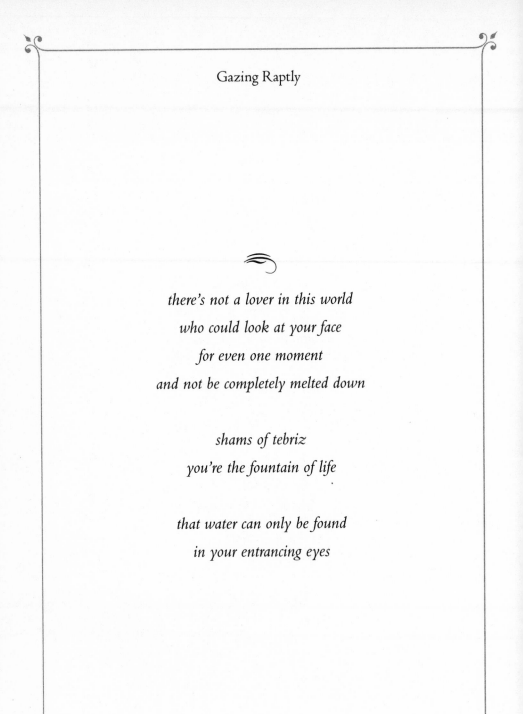

there's not a lover in this world
who could look at your face
for even one moment
and not be completely melted down

shams of tebriz
you're the fountain of life

that water can only be found
in your entrancing eyes

I need to know the secret
and learn the art
of the invisible source
of eyes and vision

look at my face
gaze at the sea of sweetness
see the waves that scatter pearls

I'm not the same me
you've seen before

Gazing Raptly

I've been gazing at your face
since early dawn

I feel reborn
you're even more beautiful than ever

you're a crazy lover
but whatever you've done in the past
it's all worth it today

I don't have enough eyes
I need hundreds more

I'd borrow them if I could
but who has the eyes
that can see you?

you call yourself a believer
but you don't know the fire
in the eyes of lovers

o one who denies
the wine on god's lips
look into my eyes

don't they look
like two glasses
full of wine?

Gazing Raptly

gaze into the face
of the one who's a reflection
of the Great Face

how incredibly beautiful!

the sun just burst from his forehead

Gazing Raptly

his eyes met mine

what do you see?
he asked

o my beautiful one
I see two wet clouds
that rain pearls

when you gaze at me
with those narcissus eyes
my soul flies out
from where I am
to the place where you've disappeared to

I used to have
thousands of knots in my heart
tied up like a sorcerer's rope

through the magic
of your beautiful eyes
they've all come undone

Gazing Raptly

the only cure
for the disease of the eye
is to get completely drunk
on the wine of the soul

and where might such a wine be found?

in the soft eyes of your friend

don't look out the window

gaze at my face instead

let it be the window
through which you look out
into nothing

you can see the beloved
by looking in his eyes

he can be found there
behind the darkness of those eyes

stay in the temple
sit by his side
look at his face

fill your eyes and heart
by looking carefully at his face

Gazing Raptly

the doctor of happiness
had good news for the lovers

every moment
a new dress for you
with fabric made of soul
he said

he gave this news with his eyes

it was like saying
there's a rope coming from the great one;
you'll soon be freed from the bottom of the well

when your gaze stops someone in their tracks
your eyes become the guide for the lost one

show him the way

put your hand on my heart
and look into my eyes

no need to ask
for wine and the drinking cup

your eyes write a new chapter
about the lessons of love

with every breath
they ask questions
suggest answers
without words
without chatter

Gazing Raptly

you are my soul
you are mine
you deserve my love
you are my light

stay in my eyes
o my eyes!
o source of life's waters

you gaze at me
and I keep looking back at you

o beauty
let's play look and see
the eyes of my soul see only you

hair hanging down
covering over the eye
is not a small thing

you need to put salve
on it immediately

when the eye is cleansed
of whatever's been covering it
you become a guide to love
just like the eye itself

Gazing Raptly

we're the ones
whose eyes and souls
have gotten all mixed up

we're the lovers
just look at us
we're out of our minds

I come to you without me
can you come to me without you?

self is the thorn
in the sole of the soul
so come
get out of yourself
merge with others

if you stay in self
you're but a grain and a drop

if you merge with others
you become an ocean

what is this light
that comes out of your eyes
and off of your face?

I wish I didn't have to do
anything else in this world
but gaze at your face

Gazing Raptly

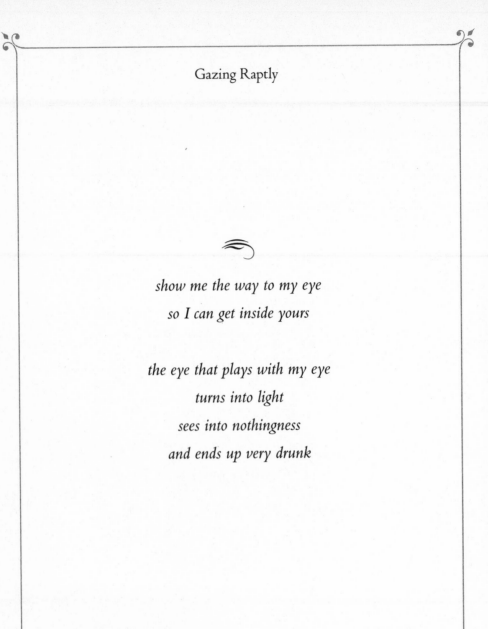

show me the way to my eye
so I can get inside yours

the eye that plays with my eye
turns into light
sees into nothingness
and ends up very drunk

Gazing Raptly

the light of our eyes
merged
with the light of the moon

you're the moon
risen in my soul;
I'm the eye

everything my eyes can see
can be repaired
or built again
but I've been completely taken apart
and melted down
by your eyes

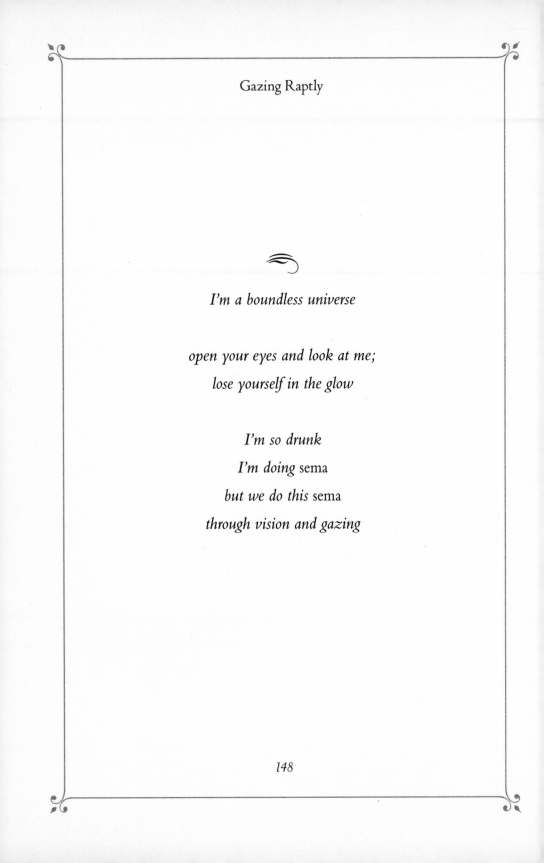

I'm a boundless universe

open your eyes and look at me;
lose yourself in the glow

I'm so drunk
I'm doing sema
but we do this sema
through vision and gazing

Gazing Raptly

o tavern keeper
serve me the red wine
that puts me in the state
where I start talking about you
and can't stop

offer me a big cup
and then watch how my drunken gaze
lets me lose myself in you

I'm looking at the place
where you turned into a river
and let me flow

that river came from the sea
and will always keep running
back to the sea

souls and eyes
went on a journey together

they finally arrived at a place so bright
that they pulled in their reins
and never again had to wonder
if the time of union
was ever going to come

lovers have heartaches
that can't be cured
by any medicine
not by rest
not by travel
not by diet
but only by seeing the beloved

meeting the friend
mends the ailment

the most important thing by far
is to gaze at the face
of the beloved

A NOTE ABOUT THE
TRANSLATIONS

*T*he translations in this book are based on three sources: the *Divan-i-Kebir,* the *Masnavi,* and the *Fiha Ma Fiha.* The *Divan* contains more than forty-four thousand verses of Rumi's spontaneously uttered poetry, and the great majority of the poems translated here comes from this source because it's here that the practices in this book are spoken of the most directly.

My source for the poems from the *Divan* is the monumental translation of the entire *Divan* from Turkish into English by Nevit Ergin. Nevit's gift to the English-speaking/Rumi-loving world cannot be overemphasized, and anyone who wants to explore the whole of the *Divan* will want to read Nevit's translations in their entirety, a task I can heartily recommend.

Rumi's other monumental work, and the one he is best known for throughout the Islamic world, is the *Masnavi,* and my versions of passages from the *Masnavi* are closely based on an abridged collection of translations into English done in 1898 by E. H. Whinfield. Rumi's skills as a master storyteller in the tradition of Jesus and Aesop are quite evident in the *Masnavi* and are represented in this book by the two delightful prose stories at the end of the section on fasting.

Rumi's only other collection of assorted writings, *Fiha Ma Fiha,* has been beautifully translated into English by Wheeler M. Thackston Jr. as *Signs of the Unseen.* The beginning of the poem that ends this book is based on a prose sentence in *Signs of the Unseen.*

BOOKS OF RELATED INTEREST

The Forbidden Rumi
The Suppressed Poems of Rumi on Love,
Heresy, and Intoxication
*Translations and Commentary by Nevit O. Ergin
and Will Johnson*

The Rubais of Rumi
Insane with Love
*Translations and Commentary by Nevit O. Ergin
and Will Johnson*

The Spiritual Practices of Rumi
Radical Techniques for Beholding the Divine
by Will Johnson

Tales of a Modern Sufi
The Invisible Fence of Reality and Other Stories
by Nevit O. Ergin

Muhammad
His Life Based on the Earliest Sources
by Martin Lings

Sufi Rapper
The Spiritual Journey of Abd al Malik
by Abd al Malik

Journey to the Lord of Power
A Sufi Manual on Retreat
by Ibn Arabi, with commentary by Abd al-Kerim al-Jili

Haféz
Teachings of the Philosopher of Love
by Haleh Pourafzal and Roger Montgomery

INNER TRADITIONS • BEAR & COMPANY
P.O. Box 388 • Rochester, VT 05767
1-800-246-8648
www.InnerTraditions.com
Or contact your local bookseller